There are many groups and organizations that have codes of conduct or ethical guidelines, some of which include:

Professional associations and societies, such as the American Medical Association, the American Bar Association, and the International Association of Business Communicators.

The American Medical Association (AMA) has a code of medical ethics that outlines ethical principles and guidelines for physicians. The current version of the AMA Code of Medical Ethics was adopted in 2016 and consists of nine sections:

Principles of Medical Ethics: This section includes foundational principles such as patient autonomy, beneficence, and non-maleficence.

Opinions on Professionalism: This section covers topics such as conflicts of interest, relationships with industry, and maintenance of competence.

Opinions on Confidentiality, Privacy, and Medical Records: This section outlines guidelines for protecting patient privacy and confidentiality.

Opinions on Communication With Patients: This section covers topics such as informed consent, truth-telling, and end-of-life care.

Opinions on Communication With Families, Friends, and Caregivers: This section covers guidelines for communicating with a patient's family, friends, and caregivers.

Opinions on Professional Responsibilities: This section covers topics such as physician leadership, advocacy, and social responsibility.

Opinions on Interprofessional Relationships: This section outlines guidelines for working with other healthcare professionals.

Opinions on Financing and Delivery of Healthcare: This section covers topics such as healthcare reform, resource allocation, and healthcare disparities.

Opinions on Research and Innovation: This section outlines guidelines for conducting research and using new technologies and treatments.

The AMA Code of Medical Ethics is intended to provide guidance and support to physicians as they navigate complex ethical issues in their practice.

The American Bar Association (ABA) has a Model Rules of Professional Conduct that serves as the basis for ethical guidelines for lawyers in the United States. The Model Rules were first adopted in 1983 and have been revised several times since then.

The Model Rules of Professional Conduct consist of a Preamble and 9 major sections:

Client-Lawyer Relationship: This section outlines the responsibilities of lawyers to their clients, including maintaining client confidentiality, avoiding conflicts of interest, and providing competent representation.

Counselor: This section outlines the role of lawyers as advisors and counselors to their clients, including providing candid advice and avoiding giving false or misleading information.

Advocate: This section outlines the responsibilities of lawyers as advocates for their clients, including representing their clients zealously within the bounds of the law and maintaining client confidences.

Transactions with Persons Other Than Clients: This section covers the responsibilities of lawyers when dealing with people other than their clients, including avoiding conflicts of interest and not engaging in conduct that could harm another person's legal interests.

Law Firms and Associations: This section outlines the ethical responsibilities of lawyers in law firms and other professional associations, including supervising other lawyers and avoiding conflicts of interest within the firm.

Public Service: This section covers the responsibilities of lawyers when serving in public positions, such as judges or elected officials.

Information About Legal Services: This section outlines the ethical guidelines for advertising and other communications about legal services.

Maintaining the Integrity of the Profession: This section covers the ethical responsibilities of lawyers to maintain the integrity of the legal profession, including reporting unethical behavior by other lawyers.

Unauthorized Practice of Law: This section outlines the ethical guidelines for the unauthorized practice of law.

The Model Rules of Professional Conduct are intended to provide guidance and support to lawyers as they navigate complex ethical issues in their practice. Each state has its own rules of professional conduct, and lawyers are subject to disciplinary action if they violate these rules.

The International Association of Business Communicators (IABC) has a Code of Ethics that provides guidance and standards for ethical behavior for its members who work in the field of business communication. The Code of Ethics consists of four principles and several guidelines:

The four principles are:

Professionalism: IABC members are committed to communication that is legal, ethical and professional.

Conduct: Members should conduct themselves with honesty, fairness, and respect for others.

Confidentiality: Members should protect the confidentiality of proprietary and privileged information.

Communication: Members should communicate accurate and truthful information to the public.

The guidelines are based on these four principles and cover areas such as conflicts of interest, relationships with colleagues and clients, the use of social media, and the accuracy of information provided to the public.

The IABC Code of Ethics is intended to provide guidance and support to its members as they navigate complex ethical issues in their profession. It is also intended to promote the highest standards of professionalism in business communication and to build trust and credibility with the public. Members who violate the Code of Ethics may be subject to disciplinary action.

Educational institutions, including colleges and universities, which often have codes of conduct for students and faculty

There are many educational institutions that have codes of conduct to guide the behavior of students, faculty, and staff. Here are a few examples:

Harvard University: Harvard's Student Handbook outlines the Code of Conduct for students, which includes guidelines for academic integrity, respect for others, and responsible behavior.

Harvard University has several codes of conduct that apply to different members of its community. Here are some of the key codes of conduct:

The Harvard University Code of Student Conduct: This code applies to all students and sets out expectations for academic and personal conduct. It covers issues such as academic integrity, respect for others, and responsible citizenship.

The Harvard University Code of Ethics and Business Conduct: This code applies to all faculty, staff, and volunteers, and sets out expectations for ethical behavior in all aspects of their work. It covers issues such as conflicts of interest, confidentiality, and compliance with laws and regulations.

The Harvard University Sexual and Gender-Based Harassment Policy: This policy applies to all members of the Harvard community and sets out expectations for respectful and professional behavior in all interactions. It covers issues such as sexual harassment, gender-based harassment, and discrimination.

The Harvard University Policies for All Faculty Members: This set of policies applies to all faculty members and sets out expectations for professional behavior, research conduct, and academic freedom.

These are just a few examples of the codes of conduct at Harvard University. Each code is designed to ensure that members of the Harvard community uphold the university's values of integrity, respect, and responsibility in all aspects of their work and personal lives.

University of California: The University of California has a Student Code of Conduct that applies to all students at its campuses, including guidelines for academic integrity, responsible behavior, and compliance with laws and regulations.

The University of California (UC) has several codes of conduct that apply to different members of its community. Here are some of the key codes of conduct:

The UC Standards of Ethical Conduct: This code applies to all UC employees and sets out expectations for ethical behavior in all aspects of their work. It covers issues such as conflicts of interest, confidentiality, and compliance with laws and regulations.

The UC Sexual Violence and Sexual Harassment Policy: This policy applies to all members of the UC community and sets out expectations for respectful and professional behavior in all interactions. It covers issues such as sexual harassment, sexual assault, and gender-based harassment.

The UC Statement of Ethical Values and Standards of Ethical Conduct for UC Students: This code applies to all UC students and sets out expectations for academic and personal conduct. It covers issues such as academic integrity, respect for others, and responsible citizenship.

The UC Academic Personnel Policies: This set of policies applies to all UC faculty members and sets out expectations for professional behavior, research conduct, and academic freedom.

These are just a few examples of the codes of conduct at the University of California. Each code is designed to ensure that members of the UC community uphold the university's values of integrity, excellence, accountability, and diversity in all aspects of their work and personal lives.

Stanford University: Stanford's Code of Conduct outlines the expected behavior of students, faculty, and staff, including guidelines for academic integrity, responsible behavior, and respect for others.

Stanford University has several codes of conduct that apply to different members of its community. Here are some of the key codes of conduct:

The Stanford University Honor Code: This code applies to all students and sets out expectations for academic integrity. It covers issues such as plagiarism, cheating, and fabrication.

The Stanford University Code of Conduct: This code applies to all members of the Stanford community and sets out expectations for ethical behavior. It covers issues such as conflicts of interest, confidentiality, and compliance with laws and regulations.

The Stanford University Policy on Sexual Harassment and Consensual Sexual or Romantic Relationships: This policy applies to all members of the Stanford community and sets out expectations for respectful and professional behavior in all interactions. It covers issues such as sexual harassment, sexual assault, and consensual romantic or sexual relationships between members of the university community where a power differential exists.

The Stanford University Faculty Handbook: This set of policies applies to all Stanford faculty members and sets out expectations for professional behavior, research conduct, and academic freedom.

These are just a few examples of the codes of conduct at Stanford University. Each code is designed to ensure that members of the Stanford community uphold the university's values of honesty, integrity, and respect for others in all aspects of their work and personal lives.

University of Michigan: The University of Michigan has a Statement of Student Rights and

Responsibilities that outlines the expected behavior of students, including guidelines for academic integrity, responsible behavior, and respect for others.

The University of Michigan has several codes of conduct that apply to different members of its community. Here are some of the key codes of conduct:

The Statement of Student Rights and Responsibilities: This code applies to all students and sets out expectations for academic and personal conduct. It covers issues such as academic integrity, respect for others, and responsible citizenship.

The Standard Practice Guide: This code applies to all University of Michigan employees and sets out expectations for ethical behavior in all aspects of their work. It covers issues such as conflicts of interest, confidentiality, and compliance with laws and regulations.

The Sexual Misconduct Policy and Procedures: This policy applies to all members of the University of Michigan community and sets out expectations for respectful and professional behavior in all interactions. It covers issues such as sexual harassment, sexual assault, and gender-based harassment.

The Faculty Handbook: This set of policies applies to all University of Michigan faculty members and sets out expectations for professional behavior, research conduct, and academic freedom.

These are just a few examples of the codes of conduct at the University of Michigan. Each code is designed to ensure that members of the university community uphold the institution's values of excellence, diversity, and social responsibility in all aspects of their work and personal lives.

Yale University: Yale's Undergraduate Regulations outline the Code of Conduct for students, which includes guidelines for academic integrity, responsible behavior, and respect for others.

Yale University has several codes of conduct that apply to different members of its community. Here are some of the key codes of conduct:

The Yale College Undergraduate Regulations: This code applies to all undergraduate students and sets out expectations for academic and personal conduct. It covers issues such as academic integrity, respect for others, and responsible citizenship.

The Graduate School of Arts and Sciences Regulations: This code applies to all graduate students and sets out expectations for academic and personal conduct. It covers issues such as academic integrity, respect for others, and responsible citizenship.

The Yale University Policy on Teacher-Student Consensual Relations: This policy applies to all members of the Yale community and sets out expectations for respectful and professional behavior in all interactions. It covers issues such as consensual relationships between faculty members and students.

The Yale University Faculty Handbook: This set of policies applies to all Yale faculty members and sets out expectations for professional behavior, research conduct, and academic freedom.

These are just a few examples of the codes of conduct at Yale University. Each code is designed to ensure that members of the Yale community uphold the institution's values of academic excellence, intellectual curiosity, and ethical leadership in all aspects of their work and personal lives.

These are just a few examples of educational institutional codes of conduct. Each institution may have its own unique code of conduct, but they generally include guidelines for academic integrity, responsible behavior, and respect for others. These codes of conduct are intended to promote a safe and positive learning environment and to help students develop ethical and responsible behavior.

Religious groups and organizations, including churches, temples, and mosques.

Codes of conduct for churches, temples, and mosques are often referred to as codes of ethics or codes of conduct for religious leaders and members. Here are some examples:

The United Methodist Church: The United Methodist Church has a Code of Ethics for pastors, which includes guidelines for professional conduct, responsible ministry, and integrity.

The United Methodist Church has a number of codes of conduct and policies that guide the behavior of its members and leaders. Here are some of the key codes of conduct:

The Social Principles of The United Methodist Church: This document outlines the church's values and expectations for ethical behavior in areas such as human rights, economic justice, and the environment.

The Book of Discipline of The United Methodist Church: This book contains the rules, policies, and procedures for the operation of the United Methodist Church. It covers issues such as clergy conduct, congregational governance, and social justice advocacy.

The Safe Sanctuaries Policy: This policy sets out guidelines for creating safe and secure environments for children, youth, and vulnerable adults within United Methodist Church settings. It covers issues such as abuse prevention, background checks, and reporting requirements.

The Code of Ethics for Pastors and Other Clergy: This code sets out expectations for ethical conduct and professionalism for United Methodist Church clergy, including issues such as confidentiality, boundaries, and sexual ethics.

These are just a few examples of the codes of conduct and policies of The United Methodist Church. Each code is designed to ensure that members of the church uphold its values of compassion, service, and justice in all aspects of their personal and professional lives.

The Catholic Church: The Catholic Church has a Code of Canon Law that outlines the expected behavior of clergy and members of the church, including guidelines for responsible ministry, respect for others, and compliance with laws and regulations.

The Catholic Church has a number of codes of conduct and policies that guide the behavior of its members and leaders. Here are some of the key codes of conduct:

The Code of Canon Law: This code sets out the rules and procedures for the operation of the Catholic Church. It covers issues such as the duties of priests and bishops, the administration of sacraments, and the governance of dioceses.

The Catechism of the Catholic Church: This document outlines the church's teachings and values, and provides guidance for ethical behavior in areas such as human dignity, social justice, and the family.

The Charter for the Protection of Children and Young People: This policy sets out guidelines for creating safe and secure environments for children and young people within the Catholic Church. It covers issues such as abuse prevention, reporting requirements, and victim assistance.

The Code of Ethics for Pastoral Ministers: This code sets out expectations for ethical conduct and professionalism for Catholic Church clergy and lay ministers, including issues such as confidentiality, boundaries, and sexual ethics.

These are just a few examples of the codes of conduct and policies of the Catholic Church. Each code is designed to ensure that members of the church uphold its values of compassion, service, and love in all aspects of their personal and professional lives.

The Islamic Society of North America: The Islamic Society of North America has a Code of Ethics for Muslim leaders that outlines the expected behavior of imams and other leaders, including guidelines for professional conduct, responsible leadership, and integrity.

The Islamic Society of North America (ISNA) has a code of ethics that guides the behavior of its members and leaders. Here are some of the key elements of the ISNA code of ethics:

Honesty and Integrity: Members and leaders of ISNA are expected to act with honesty, integrity, and transparency in all their dealings.

Respect and Tolerance: ISNA promotes respect for diversity and encourages members to practice tolerance and understanding towards all individuals, regardless of their background or beliefs.

Social Responsibility: Members of ISNA are expected to contribute positively to their communities and work towards social justice and equality.

Personal Development: ISNA encourages its members to strive for personal growth and development, both spiritually and intellectually.

Professionalism: Leaders of ISNA are expected to adhere to professional standards in their work and conduct themselves with dignity and respect.

These are just a few examples of the key elements of the ISNA code of ethics. The code is designed to ensure that members of the organization uphold its values of Islamic faith, social responsibility, and personal development in all aspects of their lives.

The Hindu American Foundation: The Hindu American Foundation has a Code of Ethics for Hindu Leaders that outlines the expected behavior of Hindu leaders, including guidelines for responsible leadership, respect for others, and integrity.

The Hindu American Foundation (HAF) has a code of conduct that guides the behavior of its members and leaders. Here are some of the key elements of the HAF code of conduct:

Integrity and Professionalism: HAF members and leaders are expected to act with integrity and professionalism in all their dealings.

Respect and Tolerance: HAF promotes respect for diversity and encourages its members to practice tolerance and understanding towards all individuals, regardless of their background or beliefs.

Advocacy for Human Rights: HAF works towards the promotion and protection of human rights, including freedom of religion, and encourages its members to be advocates for these rights.

Non-Violence: HAF promotes the principle of ahimsa, or non-violence, and encourages its members to practice peaceful conflict resolution in all situations.

Positive Contribution to Society: HAF members are expected to contribute positively to their communities and work towards social justice and equality.

These are just a few examples of the key elements of the HAF code of conduct. The code is designed to ensure that members of the organization uphold its values of Hindu dharma, social responsibility, and advocacy for human rights in all aspects of their lives.

The Sikh Code of Conduct: The Sikh Code of Conduct provides guidelines for Sikh community members, including guidelines for responsible behavior, respect for others, and adherence to religious practices.

The Sikh Code of Conduct, also known as the Sikh Reht Maryada, is a set of guidelines that govern the behavior of Sikhs. Here are some of the key elements of the Sikh Code of Conduct:

The Five Ks: The Sikh Code of Conduct requires that Sikhs wear the Five Ks, which include Kesh (uncut hair), Kara (steel bracelet), Kanga (comb),

Kacchera (special undergarment), and Kirpan (sword or dagger).

The Kacchera is a special undergarment that is one of the Five Ks, the religious articles of faith worn by baptized Sikhs. It is a specific type of underwear that is worn by both male and female Sikhs as a symbol of their commitment to their faith and the Sikh way of life.

The Kacchera is traditionally made from cotton and is designed to be comfortable and practical for daily wear. It is usually worn underneath other clothing and is meant to remind the wearer of their duty to maintain a high standard of personal conduct and to uphold the values of Sikhism.

In addition to its symbolic significance, the Kacchera is also a practical garment that serves several purposes. It provides freedom of movement and comfort during physical activity, and it also helps to maintain modesty and cleanliness. For male Sikhs, the Kacchera is also worn as a sign of their commitment to self-restraint and control over their sexual impulses. Overall, the Kacchera is an important part of the Sikh faith and is worn with pride and reverence by Sikhs around the world.

Worship and Devotion: Sikhs are required to regularly attend congregational worship and observe daily devotional practices, such as recitation of the Sikh holy scriptures.

Social Conduct: Sikhs are expected to treat all individuals with respect and dignity, regardless of their background or beliefs. They are also expected to contribute positively to their communities and work towards social justice and equality.

Personal Conduct: Sikhs are expected to uphold high standards of personal conduct, including honesty, integrity, and self-discipline.

Prohibition of Certain Behaviors: The Sikh Code of Conduct prohibits certain behaviors, such as the use of intoxicants and engaging in extramarital relationships.

These are just a few examples of the key elements of the Sikh Code of Conduct. The code is designed to ensure that Sikhs uphold the values of Sikhism, including devotion to God, service to humanity, and commitment to social justice, in all aspects of their lives.

These are just a few examples of codes of conduct or codes of ethics for religious institutions. These codes are intended to provide guidance and support to religious leaders and members as they navigate complex ethical issues in their practice and to promote the highest standards of integrity and responsible behavior in religious communities.

Athletic associations, such as the International Olympic Committee, the National Collegiate Athletic Association, and the World Anti-Doping Agency.

The International Olympic Committee (IOC) has a Code of Ethics that outlines the expected behavior of all those involved with the Olympic Games. The Code of Ethics includes the following principles:

Respect: All members of the Olympic Movement are expected to respect the Olympic values and principles.

Excellence: All members of the Olympic Movement are expected to strive for excellence in their roles.

Friendship: All members of the Olympic Movement are expected to promote friendship, understanding, and mutual respect.

Fair Play: All members of the Olympic Movement are expected to promote fair play and ethical behavior.

Human dignity: All members of the Olympic Movement are expected to respect human dignity and oppose any form of discrimination.

Sustainability: All members of the Olympic Movement are expected to promote sustainable development and protect the environment.

The Code of Ethics also includes specific rules and guidelines for members of the IOC, including rules on conflicts of interest, gifts and favors, and the protection of confidential information.

The Code of Ethics is intended to promote ethical behavior and integrity within the Olympic Movement and to help protect the reputation and credibility of the Olympic Games. Violations of the Code of Ethics can result in disciplinary action, including suspension or expulsion from the IOC.

The National Collegiate Athletic Association (NCAA) has a Code of Conduct that outlines the expected behavior of coaches, student-athletes, and other members of NCAA member institutions. The NCAA Code of Conduct includes the following principles:

Responsibility: All members of the NCAA are expected to act with integrity and take responsibility for their actions.

Sportsmanship: All members of the NCAA are expected to demonstrate good sportsmanship and respect for opponents, officials, and fans.

Ethical conduct: All members of the NCAA are expected to act ethically and in compliance with NCAA rules and regulations.

Compliance: All members of the NCAA are expected to comply with all NCAA rules and regulations.

Respect: All members of the NCAA are expected to respect the dignity and rights of all individuals, regardless of their background or beliefs.

Fairness: All members of the NCAA are expected to promote fairness and equity in all aspects of their involvement in intercollegiate athletics.

The NCAA Code of Conduct also includes specific rules and guidelines for coaches, student-athletes, and other members of NCAA member institutions, including rules on academic eligibility, amateurism, and drug testing.

The NCAA Code of Conduct is intended to promote ethical behavior and integrity within intercollegiate athletics and to help protect the well-being of student-athletes and the integrity of college sports. Violations of the NCAA Code of Conduct can result in disciplinary action, including sanctions against the institution or individual involved.

The World Anti-Doping Agency (WADA) has a Code of Conduct that outlines the expected behavior of athletes, coaches, and other individuals involved in sports. The WADA Code of Conduct includes the following principles:

Integrity: All athletes and other individuals involved in sports are expected to act with integrity and uphold the values of sport.

Fair Play: All athletes and other individuals involved in sports are expected to promote fair play and ethical behavior.

Respect: All athletes and other individuals involved in sports are expected to respect the dignity and rights of all individuals, regardless of their background or beliefs.

Anti-Doping: All athletes and other individuals involved in sports are expected to comply with the World Anti-Doping Code and all anti-doping rules and regulations.

Education: All athletes and other individuals involved in sports are expected to participate in anti-doping education programs and promote anti-doping education and awareness.

Cooperation: All athletes and other individuals involved in sports are expected to cooperate with anti-doping organizations and authorities in the fight against doping in sports.

The WADA Code of Conduct also includes specific rules and guidelines for athletes, coaches, and other individuals involved in sports, including rules on doping control, therapeutic use exemptions, and sanctions for anti-doping rule violations.

The WADA Code of Conduct is intended to promote clean and fair competition in sports and to protect the health and well-being of athletes. Violations of the WADA Code of Conduct can result in disciplinary action, including sanctions against the athlete or individual involved.

Government agencies, such as the Federal Bureau of Investigation (FBI), the Central Intelligence Agency (CIA), and the Internal Revenue Service (IRS).

The FBI (Federal Bureau of Investigation) has a Code of Conduct that outlines the expected behavior of all FBI employees. The FBI Code of Conduct includes the following principles:

Integrity: All FBI employees are expected to act with integrity and maintain the highest ethical standards.

Respect: All FBI employees are expected to respect the dignity and rights of all individuals, including fellow employees and members of the public.

Lawfulness: All FBI employees are expected to comply with all applicable laws, regulations, and policies.

Diligence: All FBI employees are expected to perform their duties with diligence and dedication.

Impartiality: All FBI employees are expected to be impartial in carrying out their duties and to avoid conflicts of interest.

Confidentiality: All FBI employees are expected to protect sensitive and confidential information and to use it only for authorized purposes.

The FBI Code of Conduct also includes specific rules and guidelines for FBI employees, including rules on gifts and favors, political activity, and use of government resources.

The FBI Code of Conduct is intended to promote ethical behavior and integrity within the FBI and to help protect the rights and interests of the public. Violations of the FBI Code of Conduct can result in disciplinary action, including termination of employment and criminal prosecution.

The Central Intelligence Agency (CIA) has a Code of Conduct that outlines the expected behavior of all CIA employees. The CIA Code of Conduct includes the following principles:

Mission: All CIA employees are expected to uphold the mission of the CIA and act in the best interests of the United States.

Integrity: All CIA employees are expected to act with integrity and maintain the highest ethical standards.

Accountability: All CIA employees are expected to take responsibility for their actions and be accountable for their decisions.

Respect: All CIA employees are expected to respect the dignity and rights of all individuals, including colleagues, partners, and adversaries.

Excellence: All CIA employees are expected to strive for excellence in all aspects of their work.

Courage: All CIA employees are expected to demonstrate courage and resilience in the face of adversity.

The CIA Code of Conduct also includes specific rules and guidelines for CIA employees, including rules on classified information, use of government resources, and relationships with foreign nationals.

The CIA Code of Conduct is intended to promote ethical behavior and integrity within the CIA and to help protect the national security interests of the United States. Violations of the CIA Code of Conduct can result in disciplinary action, including termination of employment and criminal prosecution.

The Internal Revenue Service (IRS) has a Code of Conduct that outlines the expected behavior of all IRS employees. The IRS Code of Conduct includes the following principles:

Professionalism: All IRS employees are expected to act in a professional manner and maintain the highest ethical standards.

Integrity: All IRS employees are expected to act with integrity and avoid any conduct that could compromise their objectivity.

Respect: All IRS employees are expected to respect the dignity and rights of all individuals, including taxpayers, colleagues, and partners.

Impartiality: All IRS employees are expected to be impartial in carrying out their duties and to avoid conflicts of interest.

Confidentiality: All IRS employees are expected to protect the confidentiality of taxpayer information and use it only for authorized purposes.

Diligence: All IRS employees are expected to perform their duties with diligence and dedication.

The IRS Code of Conduct also includes specific rules and guidelines for IRS employees, including rules on gifts and favors, political activity, and use of government resources.

The IRS Code of Conduct is intended to promote ethical behavior and integrity within the IRS and to help protect the rights and interests of taxpayers. Violations of the IRS Code of Conduct can result in disciplinary action, including termination of employment and criminal prosecution.

Non-profit organizations and charities, such as the American Red Cross and Amnesty International.

The International Red Cross and Red Crescent Movement has a Code of Conduct that outlines the expected behavior of all staff and volunteers working for the organization. The Code of Conduct includes the following principles:

Humanity: The Red Cross is guided by a fundamental commitment to respect and protect the dignity of all people and to alleviate human suffering wherever it is found.

Impartiality: The Red Cross provides assistance to all individuals, regardless of their race, religion, gender, or political affiliation.

Neutrality: The Red Cross does not take sides in armed conflicts or other disputes.

Independence: The Red Cross operates independently of political, economic, and military interests.

Voluntary Service: The Red Cross is a voluntary organization and its services are provided by volunteers who are committed to the organization's principles and values.

Unity: The Red Cross is a unified movement and its components work together to achieve common goals.

The Red Cross Code of Conduct also includes specific guidelines for behavior in the field, including guidelines for maintaining the safety and security of staff and volunteers.

The Code of Conduct is intended to promote ethical behavior and integrity within the Red Cross and to help protect the rights and interests of those who receive assistance from the organization. Violations of the Code of Conduct can result in disciplinary action, including termination of employment or volunteer status.

Amnesty International is a global human rights organization that has a code of conduct for all of its staff and volunteers. The Amnesty International Code of Conduct includes the following principles:

Respect: All Amnesty International staff and volunteers are expected to treat all individuals with respect and dignity, regardless of their race, ethnicity, gender, sexual orientation, religion, or any other characteristic.

Impartiality: All Amnesty International staff and volunteers are expected to be impartial in carrying out their duties and to avoid any conflicts of interest.

Non-discrimination: All Amnesty International staff and volunteers are expected to work towards the elimination of discrimination and to promote equal rights for all individuals.

Professionalism: All Amnesty International staff and volunteers are expected to act in a professional and ethical manner at all times.

Confidentiality: All Amnesty International staff and volunteers are expected to respect the confidentiality of information obtained in the course of their work.

Independence: All Amnesty International staff and volunteers are expected to act independently and free from any external pressure or influence.

The Amnesty International Code of Conduct also includes specific rules and guidelines for staff and volunteers, including rules on the use of Amnesty International resources and the avoidance of conflicts of interest.

The Code of Conduct is intended to promote ethical behavior and integrity within Amnesty International and to help protect the human rights of individuals around the world. Violations of the Code of Conduct can result in disciplinary action, including termination of employment or volunteer status.

Corporate entities, which often have codes of conduct or ethics policies for their employees.

Corporate entities often have codes of conduct to guide the behavior of their employees and to promote ethical business practices. Here are some examples of corporate entities and their codes of conduct:

Coca-Cola: The Coca-Cola Company has a code of conduct that outlines its commitment to ethical business practices, including fair competition, respect for human rights, and responsible marketing and advertising.

The Coca-Cola Company has a Code of Business Conduct that sets forth the standards of conduct expected of its employees and contractors. Here are some of the key elements of the Coca-Cola Code of Business Conduct:

Compliance with Laws and Regulations: Coca-Cola employees are expected to comply with all applicable laws and regulations in the countries where the company operates.

Integrity and Ethics: Coca-Cola expects its employees to conduct themselves with integrity, honesty, and professionalism in all business dealings.

Respect for Human Rights: Coca-Cola is committed to respecting human rights and expects its employees to respect the dignity and rights of all individuals, including employees, customers, suppliers, and communities.

Workplace Conduct: Coca-Cola has policies that prohibit discrimination, harassment, and retaliation in the workplace, and it expects its employees to adhere to these policies.

Environmental Responsibility: Coca-Cola is committed to environmental sustainability and expects its employees to act responsibly in the use and disposal of resources.

Conflict of Interest: Coca-Cola employees are expected to avoid situations that may create conflicts of interest or give the appearance of impropriety.

These are just a few examples of the key elements of the Coca-Cola Code of Business Conduct. The code is designed to ensure that the company and its employees operate with integrity and in compliance with applicable laws and regulations, and that they act responsibly and ethically in all business dealings.

Microsoft: Microsoft Corporation has a code of conduct that outlines its commitment to integrity, accountability, and respect for the law, as well as its responsibility to respect the human rights of its employees, customers, and partners.

Microsoft has a Code of Conduct that sets forth the standards of behavior expected of its employees and contractors. Here are some of the key elements of the Microsoft Code of Conduct:

Respectful Behavior: Microsoft expects its employees to treat each other, customers, partners, and competitors with respect and dignity, and to avoid any behavior that could be construed as bullying, harassment, or discrimination.

Compliance with Laws and Policies: Microsoft employees are expected to comply with all applicable laws and regulations, as well as with company policies and procedures.

Business Ethics: Microsoft expects its employees to conduct themselves with integrity, honesty, and professionalism in all business dealings.

Protection of Company Assets: Microsoft employees are expected to protect the company's assets, including its intellectual property, confidential information, and physical property.

Conflict of Interest: Microsoft employees are expected to avoid situations that may create conflicts of interest or give the appearance of impropriety.

Sustainability: Microsoft is committed to sustainability and expects its employees to act responsibly in the use and disposal of resources.

These are just a few examples of the key elements of the Microsoft Code of Conduct. The code is designed to ensure that the company and its employees operate with integrity and in compliance with applicable laws and regulations, and that they act responsibly and ethically in all business dealings.

Google: Alphabet Inc., the parent company of Google, has a code of conduct that emphasizes ethical behavior and the importance of transparency and accountability.

Google has a Code of Conduct that sets forth the standards of behavior expected of its employees and contractors. Here are some of the key elements of the Google Code of Conduct:

Respectful Behavior: Google expects its employees to treat each other, customers, partners, and competitors with respect and dignity, and to avoid any behavior that could be construed as bullying, harassment, or discrimination.

Compliance with Laws and Policies: Google employees are expected to comply with all applicable laws and regulations, as well as with company policies and procedures.

Business Ethics: Google expects its employees to conduct themselves with integrity, honesty, and professionalism in all business dealings.

Protection of User Privacy: Google employees are expected to protect user privacy and to use data only for legitimate business purposes.

Conflict of Interest: Google employees are expected to avoid situations that may create conflicts of interest or give the appearance of impropriety.

Sustainability: Google is committed to sustainability and expects its employees to act responsibly in the use and disposal of resources.

These are just a few examples of the key elements of the Google Code of Conduct. The code is designed to ensure that the company and its employees operate with integrity and in compliance with applicable laws and regulations, and that they act responsibly and ethically in all business dealings.

Walmart: Walmart Stores Inc. has a code of conduct that outlines its commitment to ethical business practices, including respect for human rights, responsible sourcing, and anti-corruption.

Walmart has a Code of Conduct that sets forth the standards of behavior expected of its employees, suppliers, and contractors. Here are some of the key elements of the Walmart Code of Conduct:

Ethical Conduct: Walmart expects its employees to act with integrity, honesty, and professionalism in all business dealings.

Compliance with Laws and Regulations: Walmart employees, suppliers, and contractors are expected to comply with all applicable laws and regulations, as well as with company policies and procedures.

Respectful Behavior: Walmart expects its employees to treat each other, customers, suppliers, and communities with respect and dignity, and to avoid any behavior that could be construed as bullying, harassment, or discrimination.

Fair Competition: Walmart is committed to fair competition and expects its employees, suppliers, and contractors to avoid any behavior that could be construed as anti-competitive or unfair.

Protection of Company Assets: Walmart employees, suppliers, and contractors are expected to protect the company's assets, including its intellectual property, confidential information, and physical property.

Sustainability: Walmart is committed to sustainability and expects its employees, suppliers, and contractors to act responsibly in the use and disposal of resources.

These are just a few examples of the key elements of the Walmart Code of Conduct. The code is designed to ensure that the company and its employees, suppliers, and contractors operate with integrity and in compliance with applicable laws and regulations, and that they act responsibly and ethically in all business dealings.

Johnson & Johnson: Johnson & Johnson has a code of conduct that emphasizes the company's commitment to ethical behavior, including transparency, honesty, and respect for human rights.

Johnson & Johnson has a Credo that serves as a guiding principle for the company's code of conduct. The Credo outlines the company's commitment to putting the needs of patients and customers first, and to operating with the highest standards of integrity and responsibility. Here are some of the key elements of the Johnson & Johnson Credo:

Commitment to Patients and Customers: Johnson & Johnson is committed to putting the needs of patients and customers first, and to developing products and services that meet their needs and improve their health and well-being.

Ethical Conduct: Johnson & Johnson expects its employees to act with integrity, honesty, and professionalism in all business dealings.

Compliance with Laws and Regulations: Johnson & Johnson employees are expected to comply with all applicable laws and regulations, as well as with company policies and procedures.

Respectful Behavior: Johnson & Johnson expects its employees to treat each other, customers, suppliers, and communities with respect and dignity, and to avoid any behavior that could be construed as bullying, harassment, or discrimination.

Fair Competition: Johnson & Johnson is committed to fair competition and expects its employees to avoid any behavior that could be construed as anti-competitive or unfair.

Protection of Company Assets: Johnson & Johnson employees are expected to protect the company's assets, including its intellectual property, confidential information, and physical property.

Sustainability: Johnson & Johnson is committed to sustainability and expects its employees to act responsibly in the use and disposal of resources.

These are just a few examples of the key elements of the Johnson & Johnson Credo. The code is designed to ensure that the company and its employees operate with integrity and in compliance with applicable laws and regulations, and that they act responsibly and ethically in all business dealings.

Nike: Nike Inc. has a code of conduct that outlines its commitment to ethical and sustainable business practices, including responsible sourcing, environmental sustainability, and respect for human rights.

Nike has a Code of Conduct that sets forth the standards of behavior expected of its employees, suppliers, and contractors. Here are some of the key elements of the Nike Code of Conduct:

Ethical Conduct: Nike expects its employees, suppliers, and contractors to act with integrity, honesty, and professionalism in all business dealings.

Compliance with Laws and Regulations: Nike employees, suppliers, and contractors are expected to comply with all applicable laws and regulations, as well as with company policies and procedures.

Respectful Behavior: Nike expects its employees, suppliers, and contractors to treat each other, customers, and communities with respect and dignity, and to avoid any behavior that could be construed as bullying, harassment, or discrimination.

Fair Labor Practices: Nike is committed to fair labor practices and expects its suppliers to provide safe and healthy working conditions, fair wages and benefits, and humane treatment of workers.

Environmental Responsibility: Nike is committed to environmental responsibility and expects its suppliers to minimize their impact on the environment and to comply with all applicable environmental laws and regulations.

Transparency: Nike is committed to transparency and expects its suppliers to disclose information about their operations and practices, including labor practices and environmental impact.

These are just a few examples of the key elements of the Nike Code of Conduct. The code is designed to ensure that the company and its employees, suppliers, and contractors operate with integrity and in compliance with applicable laws and regulations, and that they act responsibly and ethically in all business dealings.

These codes of conduct are designed to guide the behavior of employees and to promote ethical business practices. They often include specific guidelines on topics such as anti-corruption, conflicts of interest, and responsible sourcing. Violations of these codes of conduct can result in disciplinary action, including termination of employment.

Social clubs and organizations, such as the Rotary Club and the Freemasons.

The Rotary Club, an international service organization, has a code of conduct called the Four-Way Test. The Four-Way Test is a set of guiding principles that Rotarians are encouraged to apply in their personal and professional lives. The Four-Way Test consists of the following four questions:

Is it the truth?

Is it fair to all concerned?

Will it build goodwill and better friendships?

Will it be beneficial to all concerned?

The Four-Way Test is used as a guide for Rotarians in making ethical decisions and conducting themselves in a manner consistent with the values of the organization. The Four-Way Test is also used as a standard for measuring the success of Rotary projects and activities.

In addition to the Four-Way Test, the Rotary Club has a code of conduct that outlines expectations for behavior, including respect for others, integrity, and ethical behavior. The code of conduct also prohibits discrimination, harassment, and any behavior that is illegal or unethical.

Violations of the Rotary Club's code of conduct can result in disciplinary action, including expulsion from the organization. The Rotary Club's code of conduct is intended to promote ethical behavior and to guide the behavior of Rotarians in their personal and professional lives.

Freemasonry is a fraternal organization that has been in existence for hundreds of years. While it does not have a specific code of conduct, it does have a set of guiding principles that members are expected to uphold. These principles are often referred to as the "Three Great Lights" of Freemasonry and include:

The Volume of the Sacred Law (usually the Bible) - which is seen as a guide to moral behavior and ethical conduct.

The Square - which represents honesty and integrity in all dealings with others.

The Compass - which represents self-discipline and self-control.

In addition to these guiding principles, Freemasonry also has a set of values that members are expected to uphold, including honesty, respect, and charity. Freemasons are expected to be upstanding citizens who contribute positively to their communities and uphold the values of the organization.

Freemasonry also has a system of ritual and symbolism that is used to teach its members about morality, ethics, and the principles of the organization. While these teachings are not secret, they are reserved for members only and are not discussed outside of the organization.

Overall, the Freemasons do not have a specific code of conduct, but rather a set of guiding principles and values that members are expected to uphold in their personal and professional lives.

Military and law enforcement agencies around the world, such as the Royal Canadian Mounted Police and the Israeli Defense Forces.

The Royal Canadian Mounted Police (RCMP) is the national police force of Canada and has a code of conduct that outlines the expected behavior and ethical standards of its members. The code of conduct includes the following key elements:

Integrity: Members of the RCMP are expected to act with honesty and transparency, maintain confidentiality where required by law, and avoid conflicts of interest.

Respect: Members of the RCMP are expected to treat all individuals with respect and dignity, regardless of their race, gender, religion, or sexual orientation.

Professionalism: Members of the RCMP are expected to conduct themselves in a professional manner at all times, maintain their skills and knowledge through training, and uphold the law in a fair and impartial manner.

Accountability: Members of the RCMP are accountable for their actions and decisions, and must take responsibility for any mistakes or errors they make.

Courage: Members of the RCMP are expected to act with courage and bravery when necessary, to protect the public and uphold the law.

The code of conduct is designed to ensure that members of the RCMP maintain the highest standards of behavior and ethics in their work, and to promote public trust and confidence in the police force. Violations of the code of conduct can result in disciplinary action, including dismissal from the RCMP.

The Israeli Defense Forces (IDF) have a code of conduct that is based on the principle of "Purity of Arms" (Tohar HaNeshek in Hebrew). The code outlines the ethical and moral standards that soldiers are expected to uphold in the course of their duties, including:

Respect for Human Dignity: Soldiers are expected to respect the dignity of all individuals, regardless of their ethnicity, religion, or political affiliation. They are prohibited from using violence or force that is excessive or unnecessary, and must protect civilians from harm.

Honesty: Soldiers are expected to be honest in all their dealings, including in their reporting and documentation of events.

Professionalism: Soldiers are expected to carry out their duties in a professional manner, following orders and regulations, and upholding the law and military ethics.

Responsibility: Soldiers are responsible for their actions and are expected to take responsibility for any mistakes or errors they make.

Personal Example: Soldiers are expected to act as role models, demonstrating the highest standards of behavior and ethics.

Discipline: Soldiers are expected to follow orders and obey the chain of command, while maintaining self-discipline and self-control.

The IDF code of conduct is enforced through a system of military justice, and violations can result in disciplinary action, including imprisonment or discharge from the military. The code is designed to ensure that the IDF operates with integrity, respect, and professionalism, and to uphold Israel's democratic values and respect for human rights.

Online communities and platforms, such as social media networks and forums, which often have community guidelines or terms of service that outline acceptable behavior.

Here are some examples of social media networks and forums codes of conduct:

Facebook Community Standards: Facebook has a set of community standards that outline what is and is not allowed on the platform. This includes rules against hate speech, bullying, harassment, and violence.

Facebook has a set of Community Standards that outline the company's expectations for the content posted on its platform. The Community Standards apply to all users of Facebook, including individuals, organizations, and businesses. Here are some of the key elements of the Facebook Community Standards:

Hate Speech: Facebook prohibits hate speech, which includes content that promotes violence or hatred against individuals or groups based on their race, ethnicity, national origin, religion, gender, sexual orientation, disability, or medical condition.

Violence and Criminal Behavior: Facebook prohibits content that promotes or depicts violence, criminal behavior, or harm to oneself or others.

Nudity and Sexual Content: Facebook prohibits the sharing of non-consensual intimate images, as well as content that depicts sexual exploitation or nudity.

Dangerous Individuals and Organizations: Facebook prohibits content that promotes or supports dangerous individuals or organizations, including those involved in terrorism, organized crime, or hate groups.

False News and Misinformation: Facebook prohibits the sharing of false news and misinformation that could harm individuals or communities.

Intellectual Property: Facebook respects the intellectual property rights of others and expects its users to do the same.

These are just a few examples of the key elements of the Facebook Community Standards. The code is designed to ensure that the platform is a safe and respectful place for all users, and that content posted on the platform is in compliance with applicable laws and regulations, and that they act responsibly and ethically in all business dealings.

Twitter Rules: Twitter has a set of rules that prohibit abusive behavior, hate speech, and harassment. It also has policies against impersonation, spam, and violent threats.

Twitter has a set of Rules that outline the company's expectations for the behavior of its users on the platform. The Rules apply to all users of Twitter, including individuals, organizations, and businesses. Here are some of the key elements of the Twitter Rules:

Hateful Conduct: Twitter prohibits the promotion of violence, threats, or harassment against individuals or groups based on their race, ethnicity, national origin, religion, gender, sexual orientation, age, disability, or medical condition.

Violence and Physical Harm: Twitter prohibits the promotion of violence or the glorification of violent acts.

Spam and Platform Manipulation: Twitter prohibits the use of spam or the manipulation of the platform to artificially amplify content or to engage in deceptive practices.

Intellectual Property: Twitter respects the intellectual property rights of others and expects its users to do the same.

Misleading Information: Twitter prohibits the sharing of misleading or false information that could harm individuals or communities.

Child Sexual Exploitation: Twitter prohibits the sharing of content that promotes or depicts child sexual exploitation.

These are just a few examples of the key elements of the Twitter Rules. The code is designed to ensure that the platform is a safe and respectful place for all users, and that behavior on the platform is in compliance with applicable laws and regulations, and that they act responsibly and ethically in all business dealings.

Reddit Content Policy: Reddit's content policy prohibits harassment, bullying, and hate speech. It also has rules against posting personal information, spam, and illegal content.

Reddit has a set of Content Policies that outline the company's expectations for the behavior of its users on the platform. The Content Policies apply to all users of Reddit, including individuals, organizations, and businesses. Here are some of the key elements of the Reddit Content Policy:

Prohibited Content: Reddit prohibits content that promotes or glorifies violence, harassment, hate speech, and other forms of abusive behavior.

Personal and Confidential Information: Reddit prohibits the sharing of personal or confidential information without the individual's consent.

Spam and Misleading Content: Reddit prohibits the use of spam or the sharing of misleading content to manipulate the platform or to deceive users.

Sexual or Suggestive Content Involving Minors: Reddit prohibits the sharing of any content that depicts or encourages sexual or suggestive behavior involving minors.

Illegal Content: Reddit prohibits the sharing of any content that violates applicable laws and regulations.

These are just a few examples of the key elements of the Reddit Content Policy. The code is designed to ensure that the platform is a safe and respectful place for all users, and that behavior on the platform is in compliance with applicable laws and regulations, and that they act responsibly and ethically in all business dealings.

YouTube Community Guidelines: YouTube's community guidelines prohibit hate speech, harassment, and violent or graphic content. It also has rules against misleading information, spam, and impersonation.

YouTube has a set of Community Guidelines that outline the company's expectations for the behavior of its users on the platform. The

Community Guidelines apply to all users of YouTube, including individuals, organizations, and businesses. Here are some of the key elements of the YouTube Community Guidelines:

Hateful Content: YouTube prohibits content that promotes or incites hatred against individuals or groups based on their race, ethnicity, national origin, religion, gender, age, veteran status, sexual orientation, or disability.

Violent Content: YouTube prohibits content that promotes or glorifies violence or violent acts.

Harassment and Cyberbullying: YouTube prohibits content that is intended to harass, bully, or threaten individuals or groups.

Spam and Misleading Content: YouTube prohibits the use of spam or the sharing of misleading content to manipulate the platform or to deceive users.

Intellectual Property: YouTube respects the intellectual property rights of others and expects its users to do the same.

Sexual Content: YouTube prohibits content that contains nudity or sexual content that is intended to be sexually gratifying.

These are just a few examples of the key elements of the YouTube Community Guidelines. The code is designed to ensure that the platform is a safe and respectful place for all users, and that behavior on the platform is in compliance with applicable laws and regulations, and that they act responsibly and ethically in all business dealings.

Instagram Community Guidelines: Instagram's community guidelines prohibit hate speech, bullying, and harassment. It also has policies against nudity, graphic violence, and spam.

Instagram has a set of Community Guidelines that outline the company's expectations for the behavior of its users on the platform. The Community Guidelines apply to all users of Instagram, including individuals, organizations, and businesses. Here are some of the key elements of the Instagram Community Guidelines:

Hate Speech and Harassment: Instagram prohibits content that promotes or incites hatred against individuals or groups based on their race, ethnicity, national origin, religion, gender, sexual orientation, age, veteran status, or disability. Instagram also prohibits harassment, bullying, or threats towards individuals or groups.

Violence and Dangerous Organizations: Instagram prohibits content that promotes or glorifies violence or dangerous organizations.

Nudity and Sexual Content: Instagram prohibits content that contains nudity or sexual content that is intended to be sexually gratifying.

Spam and Misleading Content: Instagram prohibits the use of spam or the sharing of misleading content to manipulate the platform or to deceive users.

Intellectual Property: Instagram respects the intellectual property rights of others and expects its users to do the same.

Self-Harm and Suicide: Instagram prohibits content that promotes or encourages self-harm or suicide.

These are just a few examples of the key elements of the Instagram Community Guidelines. The code is designed to ensure that the platform is a safe and respectful place for all users, and that behavior on the platform is in compliance with applicable laws and regulations, and that they act responsibly and ethically in all business dealings.

These are just a few examples of the codes of conduct that social media networks and forums have in place to ensure that users can interact with each other in a safe and respectful manner.

Navy Seals

The Navy SEALs have a code of conduct that is based on the SEAL Ethos, which is a set of principles that guide their behavior and actions. The SEAL Ethos includes the following:

Loyalty to Country, Team, and Teammate: SEALs are expected to place the mission and the welfare of their team and country before their own personal interests.

Serve with Honor and Integrity: SEALs are expected to serve with honor and integrity, upholding the highest ethical and moral standards.

Respect for Human Dignity: SEALs are expected to respect the dignity of all individuals, regardless of their ethnicity, religion, or political affiliation. They are prohibited from using violence or force that is excessive or unnecessary, and must protect civilians from harm.

Embrace the Suck: SEALs are expected to be resilient and adaptable, able to endure and overcome adversity.

Humility: SEALs are expected to be humble and to recognize their limitations, always striving to learn and improve.

Accountability: SEALs are accountable for their actions and are expected to take responsibility for any mistakes or errors they make.

Perseverance: SEALs are expected to persevere in the face of challenges and to never give up.

The SEAL Ethos is designed to ensure that Navy SEALs operate with integrity, respect, and professionalism, and to uphold the values of the United States of America. It is a set of principles that guides their behavior both on and off the battlefield.

Army Rangers

The Army Rangers do not have a specific code of conduct, but they do adhere to the Army's values and standards of behavior. These values include:

Loyalty: Rangers are expected to be loyal to their unit, their mission, and their country.

Duty: Rangers are expected to fulfill their duty to the best of their abilities, and to put the needs of their unit and their mission before their own personal interests.

Respect: Rangers are expected to treat others with respect, regardless of their rank, race, or background.

Selfless Service: Rangers are expected to put the needs of their unit and their mission before their own personal needs or desires.

Honor: Rangers are expected to live up to the Army values and to maintain the highest standards of conduct, both on and off duty.

Integrity: Rangers are expected to be honest and truthful in all their dealings, and to maintain the highest standards of integrity.

Personal Courage: Rangers are expected to have the courage to do what is right, even when it is difficult or dangerous.

These values serve as a guide for Rangers in their behavior and decision-making, both on and off the battlefield. They are designed to ensure that Rangers operate with professionalism, respect, and integrity, and to uphold the values of the United States Army.

US Marines

The US Marines have a code of conduct that outlines the responsibilities and expectations of every Marine. The Marine Corps Code of Conduct consists of three articles:

Article I: "I am an American fighting man. I serve in the forces which guard my country and our way of life. I am prepared to give my life in their defense."

This article emphasizes the commitment that every Marine makes to serve their country and to defend the American way of life, even at the risk of their own life.

Article II: "I will never surrender of my own free will. If in command, I will never surrender the members of my command while they still have the means to resist."

This article stresses the importance of never giving up, even in the face of overwhelming odds. It also emphasizes the responsibility of leaders to protect and defend their subordinates.

Article III: "If I am captured, I will continue to resist by all means available. I will make every effort to escape and aid others to escape. I will accept neither parole nor special favors from the enemy."

This article outlines the expectations for Marines who become prisoners of war. It emphasizes the importance of continuing to resist, even in captivity, and of working to aid others in their escape.

The Marine Corps Code of Conduct serves as a guide for every Marine, outlining the values and principles that they must uphold in the service of their country. It is designed to ensure that Marines operate with professionalism, integrity, and honor, and to uphold the values of the United States Marine Corps.

Knights of the Middle Ages

The Knights of the Middle Ages were part of a noble class of warriors who served the king or lord of their region. They had a code of conduct known as chivalry, which outlined the expectations and responsibilities of a knight. The code of chivalry varied somewhat from region to region and over time, but generally included the following ideals:

Loyalty: Knights were expected to be loyal to their lord or king, and to defend their honor and interests.

Courage: Knights were expected to be brave in battle and to be willing to risk their lives for their lord or for a just cause.

Honor: Knights were expected to be honest and truthful in all their dealings, and to uphold the values of chivalry.

Courtesy: Knights were expected to be courteous and respectful to all, especially to women and the weak.

Justice: Knights were expected to be fair and just in their dealings with others, and to uphold the laws of their lord or king.

Faith: Knights were expected to be religious and to uphold the tenets of their faith.

Humility: Knights were expected to be humble and to avoid arrogance and pride.

These ideals were not always strictly followed, but they represented the ideal of what a knight should be. The code of chivalry served as a guide for knights in their behavior and decision-making, and helped to shape the culture of the Middle Ages.

Vikings

The Vikings were a seafaring people who originated in Scandinavia and were known for their military prowess and exploration of new lands. While they did not have a formal code of conduct, there were certain values and ideals that were important to Viking society, such as:

Strength: Vikings placed a high value on physical strength and were expected to be able to defend themselves and their community.

Courage: Vikings were known for their bravery in battle, and were expected to be willing to risk their lives for their people.

Honor: Vikings placed a high value on personal honor and reputation, and were expected to uphold their word and be truthful in their dealings with others.

Loyalty: Vikings were expected to be loyal to their family, their tribe, and their king.

Hospitality: Vikings were known for their hospitality towards guests, and would provide food and shelter to anyone who came to their home.

Self-reliance: Vikings were expected to be self-reliant and able to provide for themselves and their families, whether through farming, fishing, or raiding.

Exploration: Vikings were known for their curiosity and desire to explore new lands and discover new cultures.

These values were important in Viking society and helped to shape their culture and way of life. While there was no formal code of conduct, these ideals were passed down through the generations and helped to define what it meant to be a Viking.

the Bible

The Bible is a religious text that serves as a guide for the moral and ethical behavior of Christians. It contains many passages that outline the expectations and responsibilities of believers, and provide guidance on how to live a good and righteous life. Some key principles of the Bible's code of conduct include:

Love: The Bible teaches that believers should love God with all their heart, soul, mind, and strength, and love their neighbors as themselves.

Honesty: The Bible teaches that believers should be honest in all their dealings, and should not bear false witness or deceive others.

Forgiveness: The Bible teaches that believers should forgive those who have wronged them, and seek forgiveness for their own sins.

Humility: The Bible teaches that believers should be humble and avoid arrogance and pride.

Compassion: The Bible teaches that believers should show compassion and kindness to others, especially the poor and needy.

Faith: The Bible teaches that believers should have faith in God and trust in His plan for their lives.

Obedience: The Bible teaches that believers should obey God's commandments and follow His will.

These principles and many others can be found throughout the Bible, and serve as a guide for believers on how to live a righteous and fulfilling life.

Some Schools

Schools often have codes of conduct to outline the expectations and rules for behavior of students, faculty, and staff. These codes of conduct vary depending on the school and the level of education, but some common examples of rules and expectations that are included in school codes of conduct are:

Respect for others: Schools often require students to treat others with respect, including fellow students, faculty, and staff.

Bullying and harassment: Schools have rules prohibiting bullying and harassment, and often provide specific definitions and examples of these behaviors.

Academic integrity: Schools typically require students to maintain academic honesty and integrity, and prohibit cheating, plagiarism, and other forms of academic misconduct.

Attendance and punctuality: Schools often have rules regarding attendance and punctuality, requiring students to attend classes and arrive on time.

Dress code: Some schools have dress codes that specify what is and is not allowed in terms of student attire.

Substance abuse: Many schools have rules prohibiting the use of drugs and alcohol on school grounds, and may have consequences for students who violate these rules.

Safety: Schools often have rules and procedures in place to ensure the safety of students, faculty, and staff, including emergency procedures and protocols for reporting incidents or threats.

These are just a few examples of the types of rules and expectations that may be included in school codes of conduct. The specific rules and expectations will vary depending on the school and the educational level, and may be updated or revised periodically to reflect changing needs and circumstances.

Why is it important?

Ethics is important for a code of conduct because it provides a framework for the behaviors and actions expected of individuals or organizations. A code of conduct typically outlines the expected standards of behavior, such as honesty, integrity, respect, and responsibility, among others.

Ethics provides the underlying principles and values that guide these standards of behavior. It helps ensure that individuals or organizations act in a manner that is consistent with their stated values and that they make decisions that are fair, just, and responsible.

A code of conduct that is based on ethical principles can help prevent misconduct, promote ethical decision-making, and build trust and credibility with stakeholders. It can also provide a sense of purpose and direction for individuals or organizations, helping them to navigate complex situations and make choices that align with their values.

Ultimately, a code of conduct that is grounded in ethics can help create a positive culture of accountability and responsibility, both within an organization and in society as a whole.

Professionalism is important to a code of conduct because it helps to establish and maintain a certain level of ethical and moral behavior in the workplace. Professionalism refers to the qualities, behaviors, and values that are expected of professionals in a particular field or industry.

By incorporating professionalism into a code of conduct, an organization can create a framework for ethical behavior and decision-making. Professionalism can help to foster trust and respect among colleagues, clients, and stakeholders, and it can also promote a positive and productive work environment.

A code of conduct that emphasizes professionalism can help to promote integrity, honesty, and respect in the workplace. It can also help to prevent conflicts of interest, unethical behaviors, and other issues that can damage an organization's reputation and bottom line. Incorporating professionalism into a code of conduct can help an organization to operate more effectively, ethically, and responsibly.

Confidentiality, privacy, and records are important to a code of conduct because they are critical components of protecting sensitive information, ensuring compliance with laws and regulations, and promoting trust and confidence among stakeholders.

Confidentiality refers to the protection of confidential and sensitive information, such as personal data, financial information, and trade secrets. Privacy refers to the protection of individuals' rights to control their personal information and to ensure that their data is not used or disclosed without their consent. Records refer to the documentation of important information, such as financial transactions, customer interactions, and legal agreements.

Incorporating confidentiality, privacy, and records into a code of conduct can help an organization to protect sensitive information, maintain compliance with laws and regulations, and build trust with clients and stakeholders. For example, a code of conduct can outline policies and procedures for protecting confidential information, such as requiring employees to sign nondisclosure agreements and implementing secure storage and access protocols for sensitive data.

A code of conduct can also outline policies for ensuring privacy, such as obtaining consent before collecting or using personal information and providing individuals with the ability to control their data. Finally, a code of conduct can establish procedures for managing records, such as ensuring that important documentation is accurate, complete, and stored securely.

Incorporating confidentiality, privacy, and records into a code of conduct can help an organization to operate more ethically, legally, and responsibly.

Communication is important to a code of conduct because it helps to promote clear and effective communication between employees, clients, and stakeholders. Communication refers to the exchange of information, ideas, and feedback between individuals or groups.

Incorporating communication into a code of conduct can help an organization to establish clear expectations for communication among employees and with clients and stakeholders. For example, a code of conduct can outline the importance of active listening, respect for diverse perspectives, and clear and concise messaging.

Effective communication can also help to prevent misunderstandings, conflicts, and other issues that can arise in the workplace. By establishing clear and effective communication practices, an organization can promote a positive and productive work environment.

Communication is also important in reporting violations of the code of conduct. A code of conduct should clearly outline how employees can report any violations and provide them with assurance that they will be protected from retaliation. This allows for open communication and transparency, which are essential for a successful and ethical workplace.

Incorporating communication into a code of conduct can help an organization to promote effective communication practices, prevent conflicts.

Responsibility is important to a code of conduct because it promotes accountability and ethical behavior among employees and leaders within an organization. Responsibility refers to the willingness to accept the consequences of one's actions and to be accountable for one's decisions and behaviors.

Incorporating responsibility into a code of conduct can help an organization to establish clear expectations for ethical behavior and decision-making among employees and leaders. A code of conduct can outline the importance of taking responsibility for one's actions, admitting mistakes, and correcting errors.

By emphasizing responsibility, an organization can promote a culture of accountability and ethical behavior. This can help to prevent unethical and illegal practices, promote compliance with laws and regulations.

A code of conduct that emphasizes responsibility can also help to prevent conflicts of interest and other issues that can arise when employees and leaders prioritize personal gain over the interests of the organization and its stakeholders.

Incorporating responsibility into a code of conduct can help an organization to promote a culture of accountability and ethical behavior.

Interprofessional relationships are important to a code of conduct because they help to promote collaboration, respect, and professionalism among employees from different disciplines and backgrounds within an organization. Interprofessional relationships refer to the interactions and relationships between employees from different professions or disciplines.

Incorporating interprofessional relationships into a code of conduct can help an organization to establish clear expectations for respectful and collaborative behavior among employees from different backgrounds and disciplines. A code of conduct can outline the importance of active listening, respect for diverse perspectives, and effective communication practices.

Effective interprofessional relationships can help to promote collaboration and teamwork, which are essential for the success of many organizations. By fostering a culture of respect and collaboration, an organization can promote a positive and productive work environment.

Interprofessional relationships are also important for the delivery of quality care and services. When employees from different disciplines work together effectively, they can provide a more comprehensive and holistic approach to problem-solving and decision-making, which can improve the quality of care and services provided to clients.

Incorporating interprofessional relationships into a code of conduct can help an organization to promote collaboration, respect, and professionalism among employees from different backgrounds and disciplines, while also improving the quality of care and services provided to clients.

Budget is not typically considered a core element of a code of conduct. However, financial responsibility and ethical use of resources are important values that can be included in a code of conduct.

A code of conduct can outline the importance of financial responsibility, including responsible budgeting, ethical use of funds, and compliance with financial regulations and laws. It can also establish guidelines for managing expenses, avoiding conflicts of interest, and reporting financial misconduct.

By incorporating financial responsibility into a code of conduct, an organization can promote a culture of ethical behavior and accountability. This can help to prevent financial misconduct, protect the organization's assets and resources, and promote trust and confidence among clients and stakeholders.

While budget itself may not be a key component of a code of conduct, financial responsibility and ethical use of resources are important values that can be included to promote a culture of accountability and ethical behavior within an organization.

Research and innovation are important to a code of conduct because they promote the responsible and ethical use of new technologies, methods, and practices. Research and innovation refer to the development and application of new technologies, methods, and practices to improve products, services, and processes.

Incorporating research and innovation into a code of conduct can help an organization to establish clear expectations for responsible and ethical behavior when developing and using new technologies, methods, and practices. A code of conduct can outline the importance of conducting research ethically, protecting research subjects' rights and privacy, and complying with relevant laws and regulations.

By emphasizing responsible research and innovation, an organization can promote a culture of ethical behavior and accountability. This can help to prevent unethical or harmful practices.

Responsible research and innovation can help an organization to stay competitive and adapt to changing market and industry trends. By encouraging creativity, experimentation, and innovation.

Incorporating research and innovation into a code of conduct can help an organization to promote responsible and ethical behavior, while also staying competitive and adaptive in a rapidly changing market and industry.

Integrity is a core value that is essential to a code of conduct because it promotes honesty, transparency, and ethical behavior among employees and leaders within an organization. Integrity refers to the adherence to a set of moral and ethical principles, including honesty, transparency, and accountability.

Incorporating integrity into a code of conduct can help an organization to establish clear expectations for ethical behavior and decision-making among employees and leaders. A code of conduct can outline the importance of integrity in all aspects of an organization's operations.

By emphasizing integrity, an organization can promote a culture of honesty, transparency, and ethical behavior. This can help to prevent fraud, corruption, and other unethical practices.

Integrity is important for the reputation and credibility of an organization. By demonstrating a commitment to ethical behavior and accountability, an organization can build a strong reputation for reliability, trustworthiness, and high ethical standards.

Incorporating integrity into a code of conduct can help an organization to promote a culture of ethical behavior and accountability.

Duty is an important value that is essential to a code of conduct because it promotes accountability, responsibility, and ethical behavior among employees and leaders within an organization. Duty refers to the responsibility to act in a way that is consistent with an organization's mission, goals, and values.

Incorporating duty into a code of conduct can help an organization to establish clear expectations for ethical behavior and decision-making among employees and leaders. A code of conduct can outline the importance of duty in all aspects of an organization's operations, including interactions with clients and stakeholders, adherence to laws and regulations, and the responsible use of resources.

By emphasizing duty, an organization can promote a culture of accountability, responsibility, and ethical behavior. This can help to prevent negligence, non-compliance, and other unethical practices.

Duty is important for the achievement of an organization's mission and goals. By demonstrating a commitment to ethical behavior and accountability, an organization can achieve its objectives and make a positive impact on its stakeholders and society.

Incorporating duty into a code of conduct can help an organization to promote a culture of ethical behavior and accountability.

Excellence is an important value that is essential to a code of conduct because it promotes high standards of performance, quality, and ethical behavior among employees and leaders within an organization. Excellence refers to the commitment to achieving high standards of performance and quality in all aspects of an organization's operations.

Incorporating excellence into a code of conduct can help an organization to establish clear expectations for ethical behavior and performance among employees and leaders. A code of conduct can outline the importance of excellence in all aspects of an organization's operations, including product and service delivery, customer service, and internal processes and procedures.

By emphasizing excellence, an organization can promote a culture of continuous improvement, innovation, and ethical behavior. This can help to achieve high levels of performance, quality, and customer satisfaction.

Excellence is important for the reputation and competitiveness of an organization. By demonstrating a commitment to high standards of performance, quality, and ethical behavior, an organization can build a strong reputation for reliability, professionalism, and customer satisfaction.

Incorporating excellence into a code of conduct can help an organization to promote a culture of continuous improvement, innovation, and ethical behavior, while also building a strong reputation for performance and quality.

Accountability is an important value that is essential to a code of conduct because it promotes responsibility, transparency, and ethical behavior among employees and leaders within an organization. Accountability refers to the responsibility to take ownership of one's actions and decisions and to be transparent and honest about them.

Incorporating accountability into a code of conduct can help an organization to establish clear expectations for ethical behavior and decision-making among employees and leaders. A code of conduct can outline the importance of accountability in all aspects of an organization's operations, including interactions with clients and stakeholders, adherence to laws and regulations, and the responsible use of resources.

By emphasizing accountability, an organization can promote a culture of responsibility, transparency, and ethical behavior. This can help to prevent fraud, corruption, and other unethical practices.

Accountability is important for the effectiveness and efficiency of an organization. By taking ownership of their actions and decisions, employees and leaders can make more informed and responsible choices that benefit the organization and its stakeholders.

Incorporating accountability into a code of conduct can help an organization to promote a culture of ethical behavior and responsibility, while also improving its effectiveness and efficiency and building trust and confidence among clients and stakeholders.

Diversity is an important value that is essential to a code of conduct because it promotes inclusion, respect, and ethical behavior among employees and leaders within an organization. Diversity refers to the recognition and appreciation of differences in culture, background, perspective, and identity.

Incorporating diversity into a code of conduct can help an organization to establish clear expectations for ethical behavior and respect for differences among employees and leaders.

By emphasizing diversity, an organization can promote a culture of inclusion, respect, and ethical behavior. This can help to prevent discrimination, harassment, and other unethical practices, while also fostering a more engaged, innovative, and productive workforce.

Diversity is important for the effectiveness and competitiveness of an organization. By embracing diversity and respecting differences, an organization can benefit from a wider range of perspectives, ideas, and skills, which can lead to better decision-making, problem-solving, and innovation.

Incorporating diversity into a code of conduct can help an organization to promote a culture of inclusion, respect, and ethical behavior, while also improving its effectiveness and competitiveness and building a more engaged and innovative workforce.

Honor is an important value that is essential to a code of conduct because it promotes integrity, respect, and ethical behavior among employees and leaders within an organization. Honor refers to the recognition and appreciation of the inherent value and dignity of every individual.

Incorporating honor into a code of conduct can help an organization to establish clear expectations for ethical behavior and respect for individuals and their rights. A code of conduct can outline the importance of honor in all aspects of an organization's operations, including interactions with clients and stakeholders, adherence to laws and regulations, and the responsible use of resources.

By emphasizing honor, an organization can promote a culture of integrity, respect, and ethical behavior. This can help to prevent discrimination, harassment, and other unethical practices, while also fostering a more engaged, motivated, and productive workforce.

Honor is important for the reputation and credibility of an organization. By demonstrating a commitment to integrity and ethical behavior, an organization can build a strong reputation for reliability, professionalism, and customer satisfaction.

Incorporating honor into a code of conduct can help an organization to promote a culture of integrity, respect, and ethical behavior, while also building a strong reputation for performance and quality.

Respect is an important value that is essential to a code of conduct because it promotes fairness, inclusion, and ethical behavior among employees and leaders within an organization. Respect refers to the recognition and appreciation of the inherent value and dignity of every individual.

Incorporating respect into a code of conduct can help an organization to establish clear expectations for ethical behavior and respect for individuals and their rights. A code of conduct can outline the importance of respect in all aspects of an organization's operations, including interactions with clients and stakeholders, adherence to laws and regulations, and the responsible use of resources.

By emphasizing respect, an organization can promote a culture of fairness, inclusion, and ethical behavior. This can help to prevent discrimination, harassment, and other unethical practices, while also fostering a more engaged, motivated, and productive workforce.

Respect is important for building trust and relationships among employees, clients, and stakeholders. By demonstrating respect for individuals and their rights, an organization can build a strong reputation for fairness, professionalism, and customer satisfaction.

Dignity is an important value that is essential to a code of conduct because it promotes respect, inclusion, and ethical behavior among employees and leaders within an organization. Dignity refers to the inherent value and worth of every individual, regardless of their background, status, or identity.

Incorporating dignity into a code of conduct can help an organization to establish clear expectations for ethical behavior and respect for individuals and their rights.

By emphasizing dignity, an organization can promote a culture of respect, inclusion, and ethical behavior. This can help to prevent discrimination, harassment, and other unethical practices, while also fostering a more engaged, motivated, and productive workforce.

Dignity is important for upholding the basic human rights and freedoms of individuals. By recognizing the inherent value and worth of every individual, an organization can demonstrate its commitment to fairness, equality, and social responsibility.

Incorporating dignity into a code of conduct can help an organization to promote a culture of respect, inclusion, and ethical behavior, while also upholding the basic human rights and freedoms of individuals.

Honesty is an important value that is essential to a code of conduct because it promotes transparency, trust, and ethical behavior among employees and leaders within an organization.

Honesty refers to the quality of being truthful, straightforward, and sincere in all communications and actions.

Incorporating honesty into a code of conduct can help an organization to establish clear expectations for ethical behavior and transparency in all aspects of its operations.

By emphasizing honesty, an organization can promote a culture of transparency, trust, and ethical behavior. This can help to prevent fraud, deception, and other unethical practices, while also fostering a more engaged, motivated, and productive workforce.

Honesty is important for building strong relationships with clients, stakeholders, and the community. By demonstrating honesty in all communications and actions, an organization can build a strong reputation for reliability, professionalism, and customer satisfaction.

Transparency is an important value that is essential to a code of conduct because it promotes accountability, openness, and ethical behavior among employees and leaders within an organization. Transparency refers to the quality of being open, honest, and clear in all communications and actions.

Incorporating transparency into a code of conduct can help an organization to establish clear expectations for ethical behavior and accountability in all aspects of its operations.

By emphasizing transparency, an organization can promote a culture of accountability, openness, and ethical behavior. This can help to prevent corruption, conflicts of interest, and other unethical practices.

Transparency is important for building trust and relationships with clients, stakeholders, and the community. By demonstrating transparency in all communications and actions, an organization can build a strong reputation for reliability, professionalism, and customer satisfaction.

Incorporating transparency into a code of conduct can help an organization to promote a culture of accountability, openness, and ethical behavior.

Tolerance is an important value that is essential to a code of conduct because it promotes respect, inclusivity, and diversity among employees and leaders within an organization. Tolerance refers to the quality of being accepting, respectful, and open-minded towards different beliefs, values, and perspectives.

Incorporating tolerance into a code of conduct can help an organization to establish clear expectations for respectful and inclusive behavior in all aspects of its operations.

By emphasizing tolerance, an organization can promote a culture of respect, inclusivity, and diversity. This can help to prevent discrimination, harassment, and other forms of unethical behavior, while also fostering a more engaged, motivated, and productive workforce.

Self-discipline is important to a code of conduct because it helps individuals to adhere to the principles and values outlined in the code, even when faced with difficult situations or temptations.

However, simply having a code of conduct is not enough - it also requires individuals to have the self-discipline necessary to follow the code.

Self-discipline allows individuals to stay focused on their goals and values, even when faced with distractions or obstacles. This is particularly important in the context of a code of conduct, where individuals may be tempted to engage in behaviors that are not in line with the principles outlined in the code. By exercising self-discipline, individuals can resist these temptations and remain true to the values of the code.

Self-discipline helps to create a culture of accountability and responsibility. When individuals are able to exercise self-discipline and adhere to the code of conduct, they demonstrate their commitment to the values and principles of the organization. This sets a positive example for others and helps to create a culture where everyone is held accountable for their actions.

Self-discipline is a key component of any effective code of conduct. By cultivating self-discipline, individuals can better adhere to the principles and values outlined in the code.

Friendship is important to a code of conduct because it can help foster a positive and supportive culture within an organization or community, which is essential for upholding the principles and values outlined in the code.

A code of conduct provides a set of guidelines for behavior, but it is the relationships and interactions between individuals that bring these guidelines to life. Friendship can play an important role in creating a supportive environment where individuals feel motivated to follow the code.

Firstly, having strong and positive relationships with colleagues or members of a community can create a sense of belonging and loyalty to the organization or community. This sense of loyalty can increase motivation to follow the code of conduct, as individuals are more invested in the success of the organization or community.

Secondly, friendships can provide a network of support and accountability. When individuals have friends who share their commitment to the code of conduct, they can rely on each other for encouragement and support in upholding the principles and values outlined in the code. This can help to create a culture where everyone is held accountable for their actions, and where individuals are motivated to act in accordance with the code.

Finally, friendships can provide a positive influence on behavior. When individuals are surrounded by friends who are committed to following the code of conduct, they are more likely to adopt similar behaviors and attitudes. This can help to create a culture where following the code of conduct is the norm, rather than the exception.

Friendship is an important component of a code of conduct because it can help create a positive and supportive culture where individuals are motivated to follow the principles and values outlined in the code.

Sustainability is important to a code of conduct because it encourages individuals and organizations to behave in a responsible and ethical manner towards the environment, society, and the economy. By incorporating sustainability into a code of conduct, organizations can demonstrate their commitment to creating a better world for future generations.

There are several reasons why sustainability is important to a code of conduct:

Environmental responsibility: A code of conduct that includes sustainability principles can help organizations to reduce their impact on the environment. This can include initiatives to reduce waste, conserve energy, and use environmentally friendly products and practices.

Social responsibility: Sustainability principles can also promote social responsibility, by encouraging organizations to consider the impact of their actions on society. This can include initiatives to promote diversity and inclusion, ensure fair labor practices, and support local communities.

Economic responsibility: Sustainability principles can also help organizations to behave in an economically responsible manner. This can include initiatives to promote ethical business practices, such as fair competition, transparency, and accountability.

Reputation and brand image: By incorporating sustainability principles into their code of conduct, organizations can demonstrate their commitment to social and environmental responsibility. This can help to enhance their reputation and brand image, and attract customers and investors who share their values.

Sustainability is an important component of a code of conduct because it encourages organizations to behave in a responsible and ethical manner towards the environment, society, and the economy. By integrating sustainability principles into their code of conduct, organizations can demonstrate their commitment to creating a better world for future generations, and build a strong reputation and brand image based on their ethical and responsible behavior.

Sportsmanship is important to a code of conduct because it promotes fair play, respect, and integrity in sports and other competitive activities. By incorporating sportsmanship principles into a code of conduct, organizations can help to create a positive and healthy competitive environment that promotes the development of important life skills.

There are several reasons why sportsmanship is important to a code of conduct:

Fair play: Sportsmanship promotes fair play, which means playing by the rules and respecting the decisions of referees or officials. This helps to create a level playing field for all participants, and ensures that the outcome of a competition is based on skill and effort, rather than cheating or unsportsmanlike behavior.

Respect: Sportsmanship also promotes respect for opponents, teammates, and officials. This means treating others with dignity and kindness, even in the heat of competition. By promoting respect, sportsmanship can help to reduce conflicts and foster positive relationships among participants.

Integrity: Sportsmanship promotes integrity, which means being honest and truthful in all aspects of competition. This includes admitting mistakes and taking responsibility for one's actions. By promoting integrity, sportsmanship can help to build trust among participants and create a culture of honesty and accountability.

Character development: Sportsmanship can also help to promote important life skills, such as teamwork, leadership, and perseverance. By encouraging participants to develop these skills, sportsmanship can help to prepare them for success in all aspects of life.

Sportsmanship is an important component of a code of conduct because it promotes fair play, respect, and integrity in sports and other competitive activities. By incorporating sportsmanship principles into their code of conduct, organizations can help to create a positive and healthy competitive environment that promotes the development of important life skills.

Fairness is important to a code of conduct because it promotes equal treatment and opportunities for all individuals, regardless of their background or circumstances. By incorporating fairness principles into a code of conduct, organizations can help to create a culture of trust and respect that supports the well-being and success of all members.

There are several reasons why fairness is important to a code of conduct:

Equity: Fairness promotes equity, which means ensuring that all individuals have access to the same opportunities and resources. This helps to create a level playing field for all members, regardless of their background or circumstances.

Trust: Fairness promotes trust, which means that individuals can rely on the organization to treat them with respect and fairness. This helps to create a positive and supportive culture where individuals feel valued and supported.

Diversity and inclusion: Fairness promotes diversity and inclusion, which means recognizing and valuing the differences among individuals. This helps to create a culture that celebrates diversity and encourages participation from all members.

Morale: Fairness promotes high morale, which means that individuals feel satisfied and motivated in their work or participation. This helps to create a culture of productivity and engagement, where individuals are invested in the success of the organization or community.

Compliance with a code of conduct is important for several reasons:

Promotes ethical behavior: A code of conduct typically includes ethical principles and values that guide the actions of individuals within an organization or community. Compliance with these standards promotes ethical behavior, which is essential for building trust, maintaining a positive reputation, and avoiding legal and regulatory issues.

Establishes consistency: Compliance with a code of conduct establishes consistency in behavior across an organization or community. This consistency ensures that everyone is held to the same standards and expectations, which helps to prevent conflicts and maintain a harmonious environment.

Mitigates risk: Compliance with a code of conduct helps to mitigate risk by ensuring that individuals are aware of and adhere to laws, regulations, and policies that apply to their roles and responsibilities. Compliance also helps to prevent legal and regulatory violations, which can result in costly fines, legal action, and damage to the organization's reputation.

Fosters accountability: Compliance with a code of conduct fosters accountability by providing clear guidelines and consequences for non-compliance. This accountability ensures that individuals are responsible for their actions and that violations of the code of conduct are addressed in a fair and consistent manner.

Compliance with a code of conduct is important because it promotes ethical behavior, establishes consistency, mitigates risk, and fosters accountability.

Education is an essential aspect of a code of conduct for several reasons:

Awareness: Education on a code of conduct creates awareness of what the code entails and the expected behaviors. It ensures that individuals understand the purpose of the code and the principles behind it.

Understanding: Education on a code of conduct helps individuals to understand how to apply the code in different scenarios. It helps to clarify any ambiguities that may exist in the code and ensures that everyone is on the same page.

Compliance: Education on a code of conduct is critical in ensuring compliance. It provides individuals with the knowledge and tools they need to adhere to the code and make ethical decisions in line with its principles.

Culture: Education on a code of conduct helps to create a culture of ethics and integrity within an organization or community. When individuals understand and embrace the code, they are more likely to act in ways that align with its principles, leading to a positive and ethical culture.

Improvement: Education on a code of conduct provides opportunities for improvement. As individuals learn about the code, they may identify areas where it could be improved, leading to revisions and updates that reflect the evolving needs and values of the organization or community.

Education is important to a code of conduct because it creates awareness, promotes understanding, ensures compliance, fosters a culture of ethics, and provides opportunities for improvement. Without education, a code of conduct may be ineffective or not fully embraced by the individuals it is meant to guide.

Lawfulness is important to a code of conduct for several reasons:

Compliance with legal requirements: A code of conduct should reflect legal requirements and standards that apply to the organization or community. Compliance with these requirements ensures that individuals are aware of and follow applicable laws and regulations, minimizing the risk of legal and regulatory violations.

Protection against liability: Compliance with legal requirements in a code of conduct helps to protect individuals and organizations from liability. Violations of laws and regulations can result in legal action, fines, and damage to the organization's reputation. A code of conduct that reflects legal requirements can help to mitigate these risks.

Ethical behavior: Compliance with legal requirements is an essential aspect of ethical behavior. Laws and regulations are put in place to protect the interests of individuals and society as a whole. Compliance with these requirements demonstrates a commitment to ethical behavior and responsibility.

Reputation: Compliance with legal requirements in a code of conduct helps to maintain a positive reputation. Organizations and communities that are known for following laws and regulations are viewed as responsible and trustworthy.

Accountability: Compliance with legal requirements in a code of conduct establishes accountability. Individuals who violate legal requirements are subject to consequences, which may include legal action, fines, or termination of employment. Compliance with legal requirements ensures that individuals are responsible for their actions and that violations are addressed in a fair and consistent manner.

Lawfulness is important to a code of conduct because it ensures compliance with legal requirements, protects against liability, promotes ethical behavior, maintains a positive reputation, and establishes accountability. A code of conduct that reflects legal requirements helps to create a culture of responsibility and integrity within an organization or community.

A mission is important to a code of conduct for several reasons:

Alignment: A code of conduct should align with the mission of an organization or community. The mission reflects the values and purpose of the organization or community, and the code of conduct should be consistent with these values and purpose.

Direction: The mission provides direction for an organization or community, and the code of conduct should support this direction. The code of conduct should guide individuals in achieving the mission and contribute to the overall success of the organization or community.

Culture: A mission-based code of conduct helps to create a culture of shared values and purpose. When individuals understand and embrace the mission, they are more likely to act in ways that align with the values and purpose of the organization or community, leading to a positive and productive culture.

Accountability: A mission-based code of conduct establishes accountability. Individuals who violate the code of conduct are not only violating the standards of behavior but also the mission of the organization or community. This accountability ensures that individuals are responsible for their actions and that violations are addressed in a fair and consistent manner.

Reputation: A mission-based code of conduct helps to maintain a positive reputation. Organizations and communities that are known for upholding their mission and values are viewed as responsible and trustworthy.

A mission is important to a code of conduct because it aligns the code with the values and purpose of an organization or community, provides direction, creates a culture of shared values, establishes accountability, and maintains a positive reputation. A mission-based code of conduct helps to ensure that individuals act in ways that contribute to the success of the organization or community and uphold its values and purpose.

Courage is important to a code of conduct for several reasons:

Standing up for what's right: A code of conduct should provide guidance on how to act in situations that require difficult or unpopular decisions. It takes courage to stand up for what's right, even in the face of opposition or pressure.

Speaking up: Courage is necessary to speak up when something is not right or when ethical violations are occurring. A code of conduct should encourage individuals to speak up and report wrongdoing, even when it's uncomfortable or difficult.

Taking responsibility: Courage is necessary to take responsibility for one's actions, even when they have negative consequences. A code of conduct should encourage individuals to take responsibility for their actions and make amends when necessary.

Resisting temptation: Courage is necessary to resist temptation and avoid ethical violations, even when it may be easier or more convenient to go along with unethical behavior. A code of conduct should encourage individuals to resist temptation and make ethical decisions, even when it's challenging.

Upholding values: Courage is necessary to uphold the values and principles of a code of conduct, even when they are not universally accepted or popular. A code of conduct should encourage individuals to uphold these values and principles, even when it may be difficult or unpopular to do so.

Courage is important to a code of conduct because it enables individuals to act ethically and uphold the principles and values of the code, even in challenging or difficult situations.

Impartiality is important to a code of conduct for several reasons:

Fairness: Impartiality ensures that individuals are treated fairly and without bias. A code of conduct should provide guidance on how to act in a fair and impartial manner, ensuring that decisions are based on objective criteria and not influenced by personal biases or interests.

Trust: Impartiality helps to establish trust in an organization or community. When individuals believe that decisions are made without bias, they are more likely to trust the organization or community and its leaders.

Equality: Impartiality supports the principle of equality. A code of conduct that promotes impartiality ensures that all individuals are treated equally, regardless of their background, status, or relationship with the organization or community.

Transparency: Impartiality promotes transparency. When decisions are made impartially, individuals are more likely to understand the basis for those decisions and the criteria that were used. This transparency promotes accountability and helps to build trust.

Compliance: Impartiality promotes compliance with laws and regulations. A code of conduct that promotes impartiality ensures that individuals follow legal and ethical requirements and avoid conflicts of interest.

Impartiality is important to a code of conduct because it ensures fairness, establishes trust, promotes equality, supports transparency, and promotes compliance with laws and regulations.

Diligence and dedication are important to a code of conduct for several reasons:

Consistency: Diligence and dedication ensure that individuals consistently act in accordance with the code of conduct. A code of conduct should encourage individuals to be diligent and dedicated in their adherence to ethical principles and values.

Responsibility: Diligence and dedication promote responsibility. Individuals who are diligent and dedicated take responsibility for their actions and ensure that they act in ways that are consistent with the code of conduct.

Professionalism: Diligence and dedication promote professionalism. Individuals who are diligent and dedicated are committed to their work and strive to perform at the highest level of professionalism.

Ethical behavior: Diligence and dedication promote ethical behavior. Individuals who are diligent and dedicated are more likely to act ethically and avoid ethical violations.

Reputation: Diligence and dedication help to maintain a positive reputation. Organizations and communities that are known for their diligence and dedication to ethical principles and values are viewed as responsible and trustworthy.

Diligence and dedication are important to a code of conduct because they ensure consistency, promote responsibility and professionalism, encourage ethical behavior, and maintain a positive reputation.

Humanity is important to a code of conduct for several reasons:

Respect: Humanity ensures that individuals are treated with respect and dignity. A code of conduct should promote respect for all individuals, regardless of their background or status.

Compassion: Humanity promotes compassion. A code of conduct should encourage individuals to act with empathy and compassion towards others, particularly those who are vulnerable or marginalized.

Diversity: Humanity supports diversity. A code of conduct should promote diversity and inclusion, recognizing the value of different perspectives and experiences.

Responsibility: Humanity promotes responsibility. A code of conduct should encourage individuals to take responsibility for their actions and their impact on others.

Ethics: Humanity promotes ethical behavior. A code of conduct that promotes humanity ensures that individuals act in ways that are consistent with ethical principles and values.

Humanity is important to a code of conduct because it promotes respect, compassion, diversity, responsibility, and ethical behavior. A code of conduct that incorporates humanity can help to create a culture of empathy and responsibility within an organization or community, promoting positive relationships and a sense of social responsibility.

Neutrality is important to a code of conduct for several reasons:

Impartiality: Neutrality promotes impartiality. A code of conduct should encourage individuals to remain neutral and avoid taking sides, particularly in situations where conflicts of interest or bias may be present.

Objectivity: Neutrality supports objectivity. A code of conduct should encourage individuals to base their decisions on objective criteria and avoid being influenced by personal biases or interests.

Fairness: Neutrality promotes fairness. A code of conduct should ensure that all individuals are treated fairly and without bias, regardless of their background, status, or relationship with the organization or community.

Consistency: Neutrality ensures consistency. A code of conduct should ensure that individuals consistently act in accordance with ethical principles and values, without regard to personal interests or biases.

Trust: Neutrality helps to establish trust. When individuals believe that decisions are made without bias, they are more likely to trust the organization or community and its leaders.

Neutrality is important to a code of conduct because it promotes impartiality, objectivity, fairness, consistency, and trust.

Independence is important to a code of conduct for several reasons:

Integrity: Independence promotes integrity. A code of conduct should encourage individuals to act with integrity and avoid conflicts of interest or personal biases.

Objectivity: Independence supports objectivity. A code of conduct should encourage individuals to base their decisions on objective criteria and avoid being influenced by personal interests or outside pressures.

Accountability: Independence promotes accountability. A code of conduct should ensure that individuals take responsibility for their actions and decisions, without being unduly influenced by outside parties.

Transparency: Independence supports transparency. A code of conduct should ensure that decisions are made openly and transparently, without hidden biases or outside pressures.

Trust: Independence helps to establish trust. When individuals believe that decisions are made independently and without undue influence, they are more likely to trust the organization or community and its leaders.

Independence is important to a code of conduct because it promotes integrity, objectivity, accountability, transparency, and trust.

Unity is important to a code of conduct for several reasons:

Collaboration: Unity promotes collaboration. A code of conduct should encourage individuals to work together towards common goals, sharing resources and knowledge to achieve the best possible outcomes.

Shared values: Unity supports shared values. A code of conduct should ensure that all individuals share common values and principles, promoting a sense of unity and purpose.

Consistency: Unity ensures consistency. A code of conduct should ensure that individuals consistently act in accordance with shared values and principles, promoting a culture of integrity and responsibility.

Support: Unity promotes support. A code of conduct should encourage individuals to support each other in achieving shared goals, promoting a sense of community and responsibility.

Reputation: Unity helps to maintain a positive reputation. Organizations and communities that are known for their unity and collaboration are viewed as responsible and trustworthy.

Unity is important to a code of conduct because it promotes collaboration, shared values, consistency, support, and a positive reputation.

Non-discrimination is important to a code of conduct for several reasons:

Equality: Non-discrimination promotes equality. A code of conduct should ensure that all individuals are treated equally and without bias, regardless of their background, status, or identity.

Diversity: Non-discrimination supports diversity. A code of conduct should promote diversity and inclusion, recognizing the value of different perspectives and experiences.

Respect: Non-discrimination promotes respect. A code of conduct should encourage individuals to respect each other's differences and avoid discriminatory behavior.

Ethics: Non-discrimination promotes ethical behavior. A code of conduct that promotes non-discrimination ensures that individuals act in ways that are consistent with ethical principles and values.

Legal compliance: Non-discrimination is often required by law. A code of conduct should ensure that individuals comply with relevant laws and regulations related to discrimination.

Non-discrimination is important to a code of conduct because it promotes equality, diversity, respect, ethical behavior, and legal compliance.

Fair competition is important to a code of conduct for several reasons:

Ethics: Fair competition promotes ethical behavior. A code of conduct should encourage individuals to act with integrity and avoid unfair or deceptive practices.

Innovation: Fair competition promotes innovation. A code of conduct should encourage individuals to develop new and better products, services, and processes, promoting innovation and creativity.

Consumer protection: Fair competition protects consumers. A code of conduct should ensure that consumers are not subjected to unfair or deceptive practices, and that they have access to quality products and services.

Legal compliance: Fair competition is often required by law. A code of conduct should ensure that individuals comply with relevant laws and regulations related to fair competition.

Trust: Fair competition helps to establish trust. When individuals believe that competition is fair, they are more likely to trust the organization or community and its leaders.

Fair competition is important to a code of conduct because it promotes ethics, innovation, consumer protection, legal compliance, and trust.

Commitment is important to a code of conduct for several reasons:

Accountability: Commitment promotes accountability. A code of conduct should ensure that individuals are held accountable for their actions and that they take responsibility for their behavior.

Consistency: Commitment ensures consistency. A code of conduct should ensure that individuals consistently act in accordance with shared values and principles, promoting a culture of integrity and responsibility.

Trust: Commitment helps to establish trust. When individuals demonstrate a commitment to shared values and principles, they are more likely to be trusted by others.

Reputation: Commitment helps to maintain a positive reputation. Organizations and communities that are known for their commitment to shared values and principles are viewed as responsible and trustworthy.

Perseverance: Commitment promotes perseverance. A code of conduct should encourage individuals to persist in the face of challenges, promoting a culture of resilience and determination.

Commitment is important to a code of conduct because it promotes accountability, consistency, trust, reputation, and perseverance.

Asset protection is important to a code of conduct for several reasons:

Responsibility: Asset protection promotes responsibility. A code of conduct should ensure that individuals take responsibility for protecting the assets of the organization or community, including physical assets, intellectual property, and other resources.

Sustainability: Asset protection promotes sustainability. A code of conduct should ensure that assets are managed in a way that promotes long-term sustainability and avoids waste or misuse.

Risk management: Asset protection helps to manage risk. A code of conduct should ensure that individuals identify and mitigate risks to assets, promoting a culture of risk management and preparedness.

Reputation: Asset protection helps to maintain a positive reputation. Organizations and communities that are known for their responsible management of assets are viewed as trustworthy and reliable.

Legal compliance: Asset protection is often required by law. A code of conduct should ensure that individuals comply with relevant laws and regulations related to asset protection.

Asset protection is important to a code of conduct because it promotes responsibility, sustainability, risk management, reputation, and legal compliance.

Personal example is important to a code of conduct for several reasons:

Leadership: Personal example promotes leadership. A code of conduct should ensure that individuals in leadership positions lead by example, modeling the behavior they expect from others.

Accountability: Personal example promotes accountability. A code of conduct should ensure that individuals are held accountable for their behavior, and that they take responsibility for setting a positive example for others.

Trust: Personal example helps to establish trust. When individuals in leadership positions demonstrate a commitment to shared values and principles, they are more likely to be trusted by others.

Culture: Personal example shapes organizational or community culture. A code of conduct should ensure that individuals set the tone for the organization or community, promoting a culture of integrity, responsibility, and positive social values.

Learning: Personal example provides a learning opportunity. A code of conduct should encourage individuals to learn from the positive examples of others, promoting personal and professional development.

Personal example is important to a code of conduct because it promotes leadership, accountability, trust, culture, and learning.

Loyalty is important to a code of conduct for several reasons:

Trust: Loyalty promotes trust. A code of conduct should ensure that individuals demonstrate loyalty to the organization or community, fostering a sense of trust and commitment.

Teamwork: Loyalty promotes teamwork. A code of conduct should ensure that individuals work together to achieve common goals, promoting a culture of collaboration and mutual support.

Accountability: Loyalty promotes accountability. A code of conduct should ensure that individuals are held accountable for their actions, and that they take responsibility for their behavior in the context of the organization or community.

Reputation: Loyalty helps to maintain a positive reputation. Organizations and communities that are known for their loyalty and commitment to their values and principles are viewed as responsible and trustworthy.

Resilience: Loyalty promotes resilience. A code of conduct should encourage individuals to persist in the face of challenges and adversity, promoting a culture of perseverance and determination.

Loyalty is important to a code of conduct because it promotes trust, teamwork, accountability, reputation, and resilience. A code of conduct that incorporates loyalty can help to create a culture of responsible commitment and positive social values within an organization or community, promoting positive relationships and a sense of social responsibility. However, it is important to note that loyalty should not override ethical or legal obligations, and individuals should always prioritize integrity and responsibility over blind loyalty to the organization or community.

Humility is important to a code of conduct for several reasons:

Respect: Humility promotes respect. A code of conduct should ensure that individuals demonstrate humility and respect for others, regardless of their position or status within the organization or community.

Learning: Humility promotes learning. A code of conduct should encourage individuals to be open to feedback and willing to learn from their mistakes, promoting personal and professional development.

Collaboration: Humility promotes collaboration. A code of conduct should ensure that individuals are willing to work together and contribute their strengths to achieve common goals, promoting a culture of teamwork and mutual support.

Accountability: Humility promotes accountability. A code of conduct should ensure that individuals take responsibility for their actions, and that they are willing to admit when they are wrong or have made a mistake.

Self-awareness: Humility promotes self-awareness. A code of conduct should encourage individuals to reflect on their own strengths and weaknesses, promoting a culture of self-improvement and personal growth.

Humility is important to a code of conduct because it promotes respect, learning, collaboration, accountability, and self-awareness.

Perseverance is important to a code of conduct for several reasons:

Commitment: Perseverance promotes commitment. A code of conduct should ensure that individuals are committed to their goals and values, and that they persist in the face of challenges and adversity.

Responsibility: Perseverance promotes responsibility. A code of conduct should ensure that individuals take responsibility for their actions and are accountable for their behavior, even when faced with obstacles.

Growth: Perseverance promotes personal and professional growth. A code of conduct should encourage individuals to continue learning and improving, even when faced with setbacks or failures.

Resilience: Perseverance promotes resilience. A code of conduct should ensure that individuals are able to bounce back from setbacks and failures, and that they are able to maintain a positive attitude even in difficult circumstances.

Innovation: Perseverance promotes innovation. A code of conduct should encourage individuals to think creatively and develop new solutions to problems, even when faced with obstacles or constraints.

Perseverance is important to a code of conduct because it promotes commitment, responsibility, growth, resilience, and innovation.

Selfless service is important to a code of conduct for several reasons:

Community: Selfless service promotes a sense of community. A code of conduct should ensure that individuals are committed to serving others and contributing to the greater good, rather than solely focusing on their own self-interest.

Responsibility: Selfless service promotes responsibility. A code of conduct should ensure that individuals take responsibility for the well-being of others and are committed to helping others when needed.

Empathy: Selfless service promotes empathy. A code of conduct should ensure that individuals are able to understand and relate to the needs of others, and are willing to put the needs of others before their own.

Leadership: Selfless service promotes leadership. A code of conduct should encourage individuals to lead by example and to inspire others through their acts of service and dedication.

Integrity: Selfless service promotes integrity. A code of conduct should ensure that individuals act with honesty and transparency, and that they do not use their position of power or influence for personal gain.

Selfless service is important to a code of conduct because it promotes a sense of community, responsibility, empathy, leadership, and integrity.

Summery

We discussed various codes of conduct followed by different organizations, institutions, and groups. We talked about examples of codes of conduct for various entities, including the American Medical Association, American Bar Association, International Association of Business Communicators, Churches, Temples and Mosques, International Olympic Committee, National Collegiate Athletic Association, World Anti-Doping Agency, FBI, CIA, IRS, Red Cross, Amnesty International, Corporations, Rotary Club, Freemasons, Royal Canadian Mounted Police, Israeli Defense Forces, social media networks, forums, and schools. We also briefly mentioned some common themes and expectations included in codes of conduct, such as respect for others, academic integrity, safety, and rules regarding attendance and punctuality.